ASTRONOMY COLORING AND ACTIVITY BOOK For Kids

70 COLORING PAGES, DOT-TO-DOTS, MAZES, AND MORE

CAP Saucier, MS

ROCKRIDGE PRESS

Copyright © 2022 by Rockridge Press, Oakland, California

No part of this publication may be reproduced, stored in a retrieval system, or transmitted in any form or by any means, electronic, mechanical, photocopying, recording, scanning, or otherwise, except as permitted under Sections 107 or 108 of the 1976 United States Copyright Act, without the prior written permission of the Publisher. Requests to the Publisher for permission should be addressed to the Permissions Department, Rockridge Press, 1955 Broadway, Suite 400, Oakland, CA 94612.

Limit of Liability/Disclaimer of Warranty: The Publisher and the author make no representations or warranties with respect to the accuracy or completeness of the contents of this work and specifically disclaim all warranties, including without limitation warranties of fitness for a particular purpose. No warranty may be created or extended by sales or promotional materials. The advice and strategies contained herein may not be suitable for every situation. This work is sold with the understanding that the Publisher is not engaged in rendering medical, legal, or other professional advice or services. If professional assistance is required, the services of a competent professional person should be sought. Neither the Publisher nor the author shall be liable for damages arising herefrom. The fact that an individual, organization, or website is referred to in this work as a citation and/or potential source of further information does not mean that the author or the Publisher endorses the information the individual, organization, or website may provide or recommendations they/it may make. Further, readers should be aware that websites listed in this work may have changed or disappeared between when this work was written and when it is read.

For general information on our other products and services or to obtain technical support, please contact our Customer Care Department within the United States at (866) 744-2665, or outside the United States at (510) 253-0500.

Rockridge Press publishes its books in a variety of electronic and print formats. Some content that appears in print may not be available in electronic books, and vice versa.

TRADEMARKS: Rockridge Press and the Rockridge Press logo are trademarks or registered trademarks of Callisto Media Inc. and/or its affiliates, in the United States and other countries, and may not be used without written permission. All other trademarks are the property of their respective owners. Rockridge Press is not associated with any product or vendor mentioned in this book.

Interior and Cover Designer: Tricia Jang
Art Producer: Sue Bischofberger
Editor: Jeanann Pannasch
Production Editor: Holland Baker
Production Manager: Holly Haydash

Illustration © 2022 Collaborate Agency

Paperback ISBN: 978-1-63878-386-2
R0

WELCOME TO SPACE!

When you look up at the night sky, does it make you feel small? With so many stars and planets shining in the black sky, you can tell that space is huge. The universe contains space and everything else in it. You are part of the universe, too!

Astronomy is the study of space. On the next pages, you will get to learn about stars, planets, space scientists, and more. Use crayons or colored pencils to color the cool art and finish the fun activities. You'll even get to help a Mars rover reach a crater! Are you ready?

Countdown: 10, 9, 8, 7, 6, 5, 4, 3, 2, 1. . .

BLAST OFF!

Where Is Our Solar System?

Our solar system is in the Milky Way Galaxy.
It is off to one side of the galaxy.
Connect the dots to find Earth and our sun.

See page 72 for the answer key.

About Our Solar System

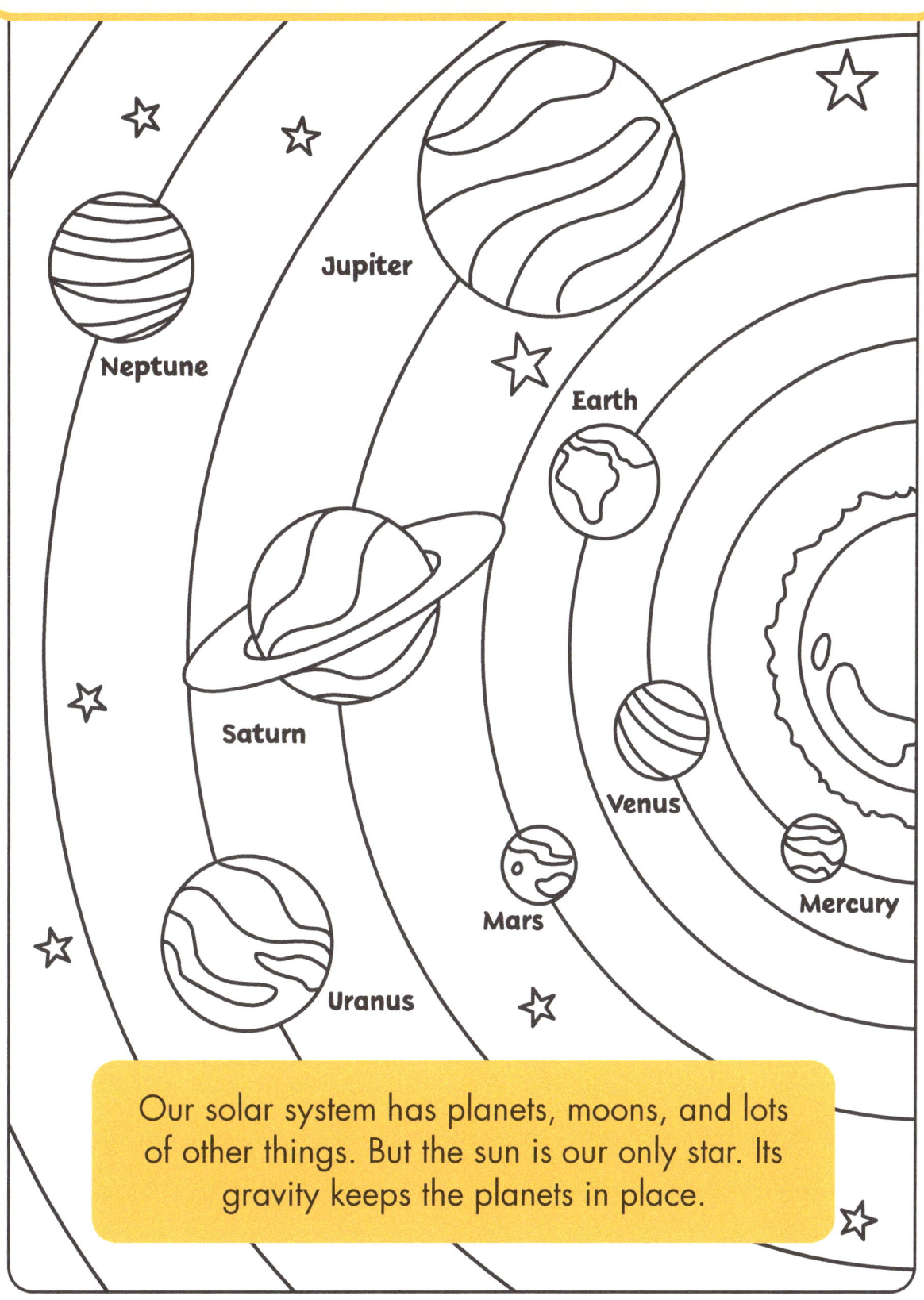

Our solar system has planets, moons, and lots of other things. But the sun is our only star. Its gravity keeps the planets in place.

Space Travel

Machines, such as robots, orbit other planets to give us information. An orbit is the path around another object. Match the words with the clues to complete the puzzle.

**ROCKET   EXPLORE   PATH   COUNTDOWN
PLANETS   MARS   FLY   MISSION**

ACROSS
2. Rovers explore this planet
5. To travel into the sky
6. Counting backward before a rocket launches
7. To go somewhere new and find out what is there
8. An orbit is a _____ around something

DOWN
1. A plan to visit another planet
3. Eight round objects that orbit the sun
4. A machine that blasts off into space

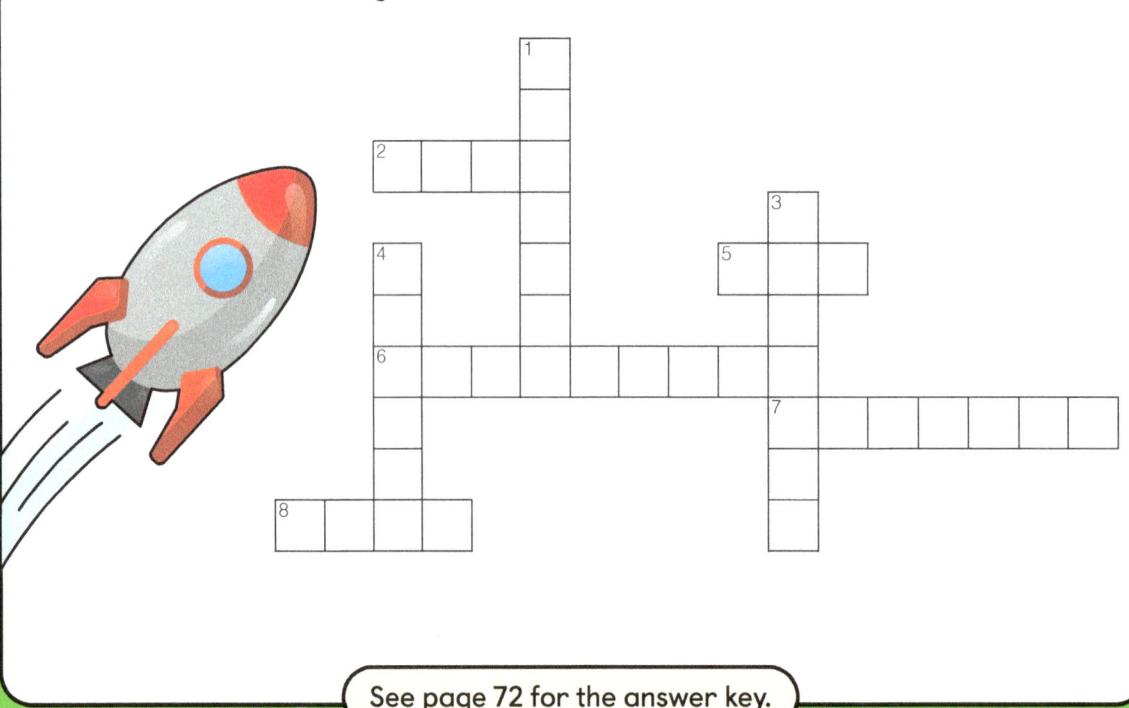

See page 72 for the answer key.

We Are Part of the Universe

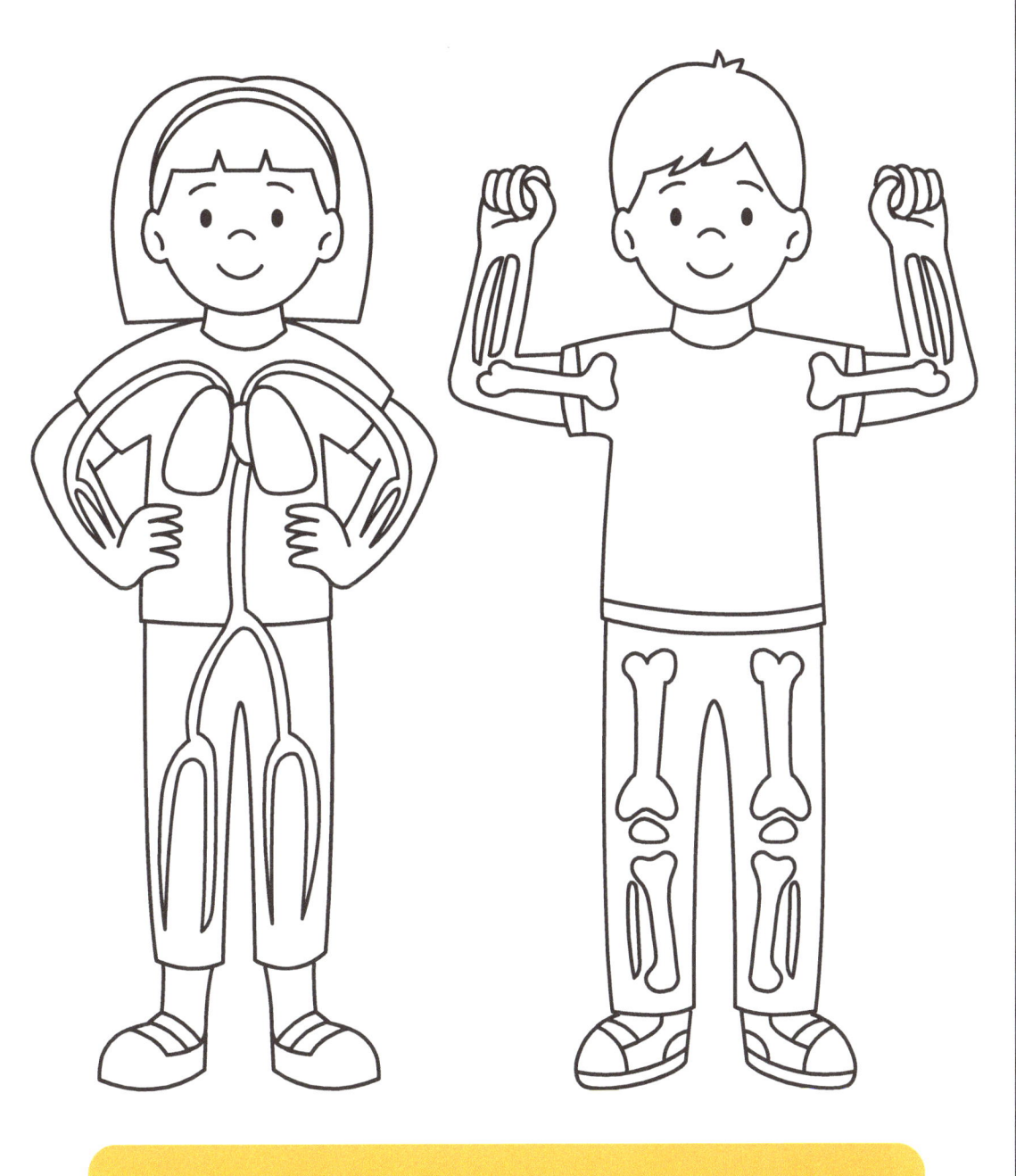

Many elements come from exploding stars far out in space. These elements are part of our bodies. They give us calcium, iron, and oxygen.

How to Get to Mars

It takes nine months to get to Mars. Help these astronauts find their way in the spaceship from Earth to Mars.

See page 72 for the answer key.

What Is a Comet?

A comet is sometimes called a "dirty snowball." It is made of dust, ice, and frozen gas.

A Spiral Galaxy

We live in the Milky Way Galaxy. It is shaped like a spiral. Other galaxies are different shapes.

Circle the galaxy words in the puzzle. Look left to right, top to bottom, and diagonally.

**ASTEROID   OVAL   COMET   GALAXY   GRAVITY
METEOR   MOONS   SPIRAL   STAR   SUN**

J	P	D	Q	X	M	D	M	G	K	C	M
W	Q	H	W	R	T	E	L	X	H	V	L
O	Q	K	T	P	I	S	T	T	N	A	F
U	V	C	E	N	V	X	Y	E	R	G	G
X	L	A	M	F	U	X	L	I	O	J	N
T	Q	X	L	J	A	S	P	J	O	R	D
X	M	Z	C	L	R	S	T	A	R	L	U
U	O	X	A	X	G	R	A	V	I	T	Y
Q	O	G	E	B	F	X	M	N	C	H	S
B	N	O	K	C	O	M	E	T	E	X	U
A	S	T	E	R	O	I	D	Z	U	M	N
G	S	I	C	C	T	E	M	P	R	S	N

See page 72 for the answer key.

Rocks Fall from the Sky

An asteroid is a chunk of rock or metal in space. Scientists believe that one fell from the sky millions of years ago. It killed most of the dinosaurs.

Eyes in Space

A satellite is an object that orbits a planet. Our moon is a satellite. Humans make satellites to do a lot of work. They help people watch television and check the weather. Match the words with the clues to complete the puzzle.

MOON   WEATHER   SATELLITE
PLANET   TELEVISION   SUN

ACROSS

3. Humans make satellites to help us watch this
6. A round object that orbits the sun

DOWN

1. Object that orbits a planet
2. Some satellites check rain and storms, which are called this.
4. Center of the solar system
5. Earth's natural satellite

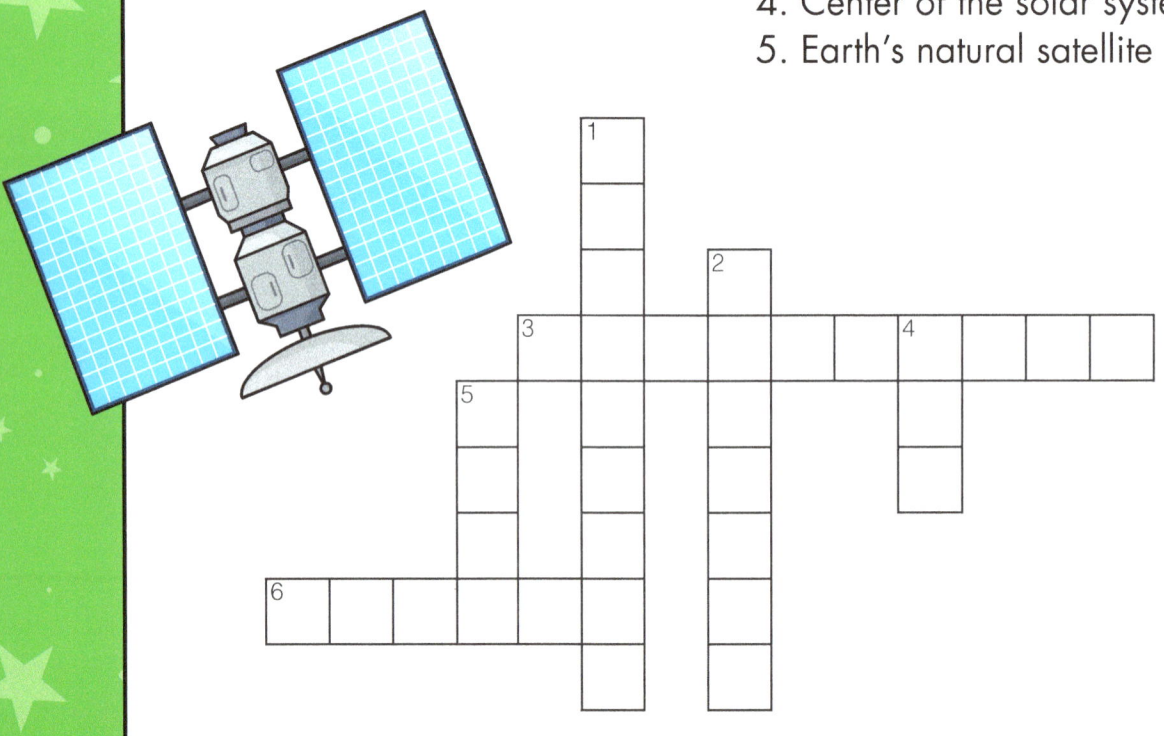

See page 72 for the answer key.

The First American Woman Astronaut

Sally Ride was an astronaut and physicist. She became the first American woman to fly into space. She traveled on the space shuttle *Challenger* in 1983.

The First American Person of Color in Space

Guion "Guy" Bluford was the first African American to go to space. Help him find his way to the space shuttle launch pad.

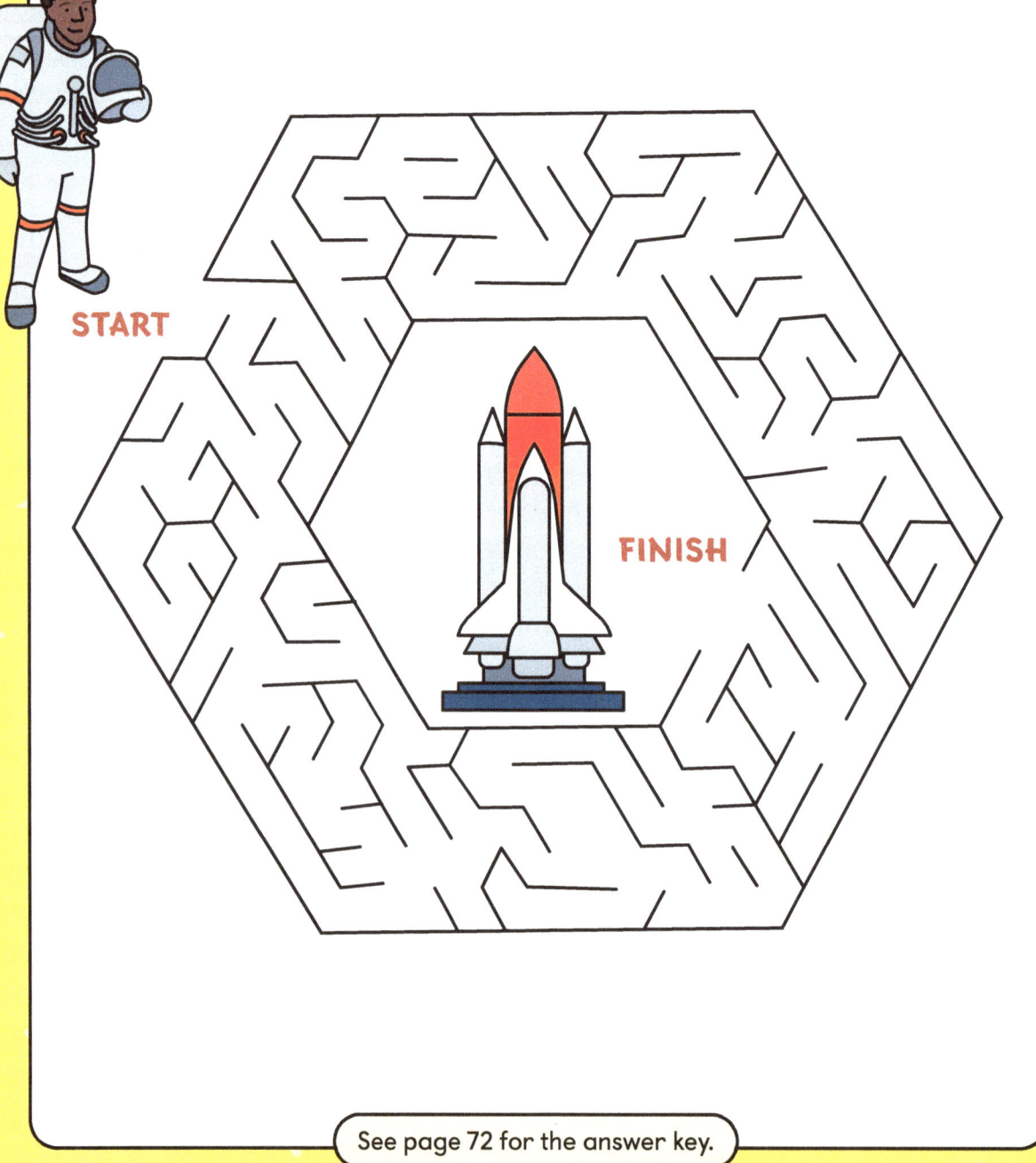

See page 72 for the answer key.

A Shower of Meteors

Have you ever seen a shooting star in the night sky? It's not a star; it's a meteor. That's a small piece of space rock burning up in Earth's atmosphere.

Eyes in the Skies

Telescopes let us see far into space. They show us things that we didn't know were there. Circle the parts of a telescope in the puzzle. Look left to right, top to bottom, and diagonally.

**EYEPIECE   FOCUSER   TRIPOD   TUBE   LENS
MIRROR   MOUNT   FINDER**

M	G	R	M	Q	N	T	D	R	X
G	H	F	C	I	U	V	E	V	X
N	W	C	O	B	R	D	Z	M	W
T	M	Z	A	C	N	R	D	R	K
R	O	J	O	I	U	Z	O	M	B
I	U	T	F	F	G	S	K	R	R
P	N	E	Y	E	P	I	E	C	E
O	T	B	S	P	O	J	I	R	D
D	N	F	I	T	U	B	E	Y	R
L	E	N	S	M	T	A	V	U	P

See page 72 for the answer key.

Sights Far Away

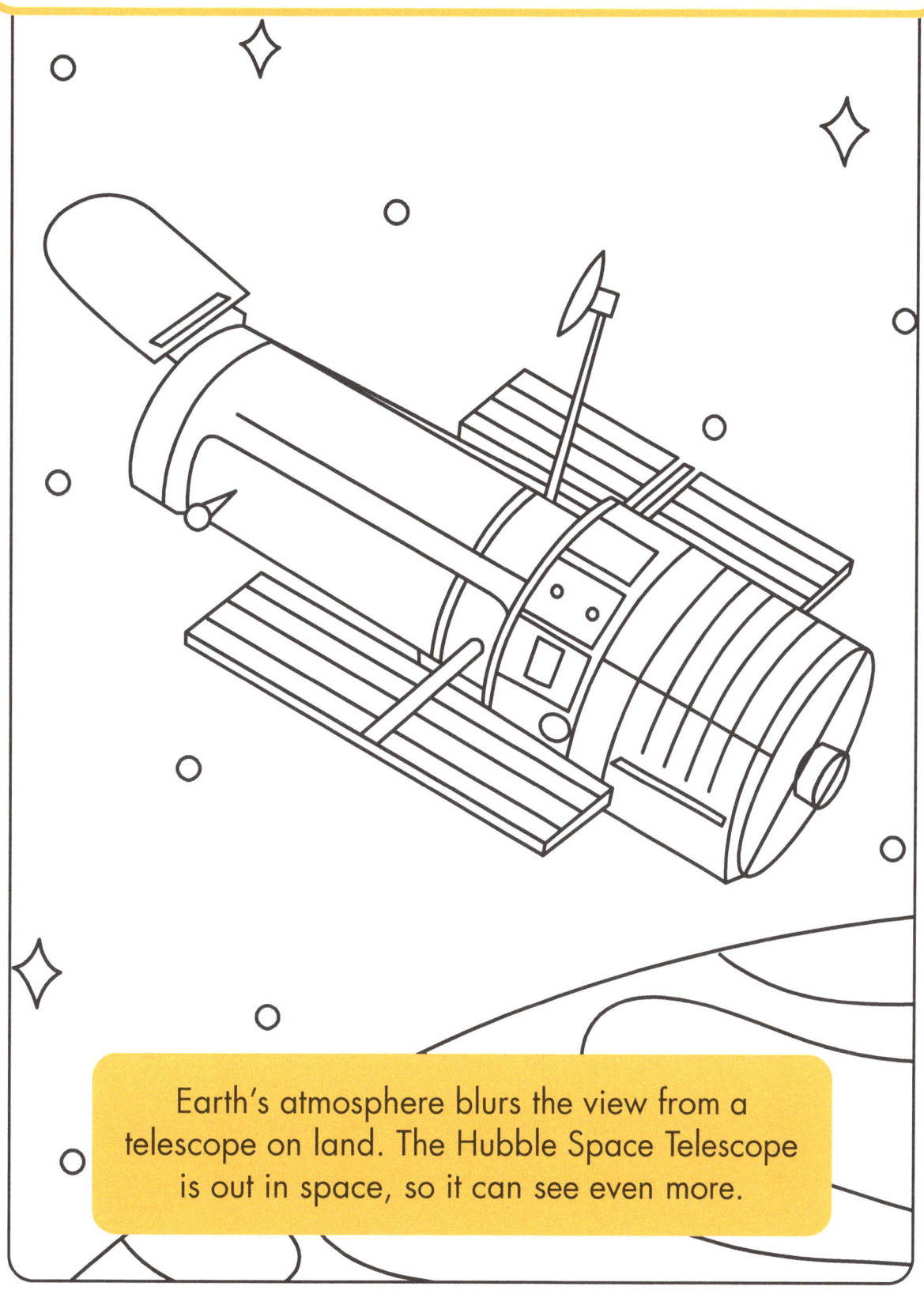

Earth's atmosphere blurs the view from a telescope on land. The Hubble Space Telescope is out in space, so it can see even more.

Look Even Farther!

The James Webb Space Telescope launched on December 25, 2021. It is more powerful than Hubble. Its mirrors are covered in gold! Connect the dots to see how the sunshields are layered under the mirror.

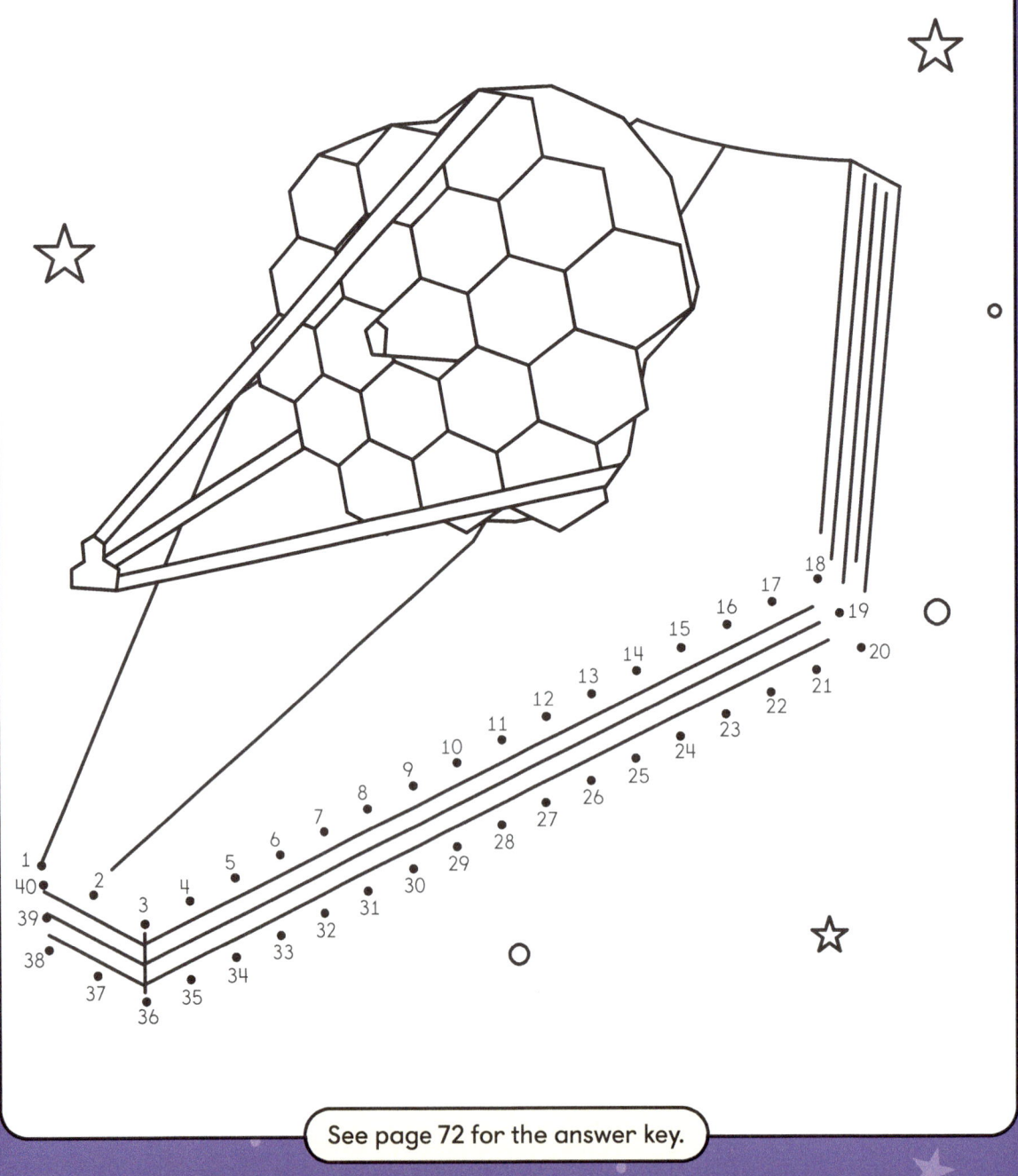

See page 72 for the answer key.

How Big Is the Sun?

The sun is one million times bigger than Earth. Its light takes eight minutes to reach Earth. All the planets could fit inside the sun.

Roving Over Mars

NASA sent robot rovers to look for water and signs of life on Mars. The rovers explore Mars until humans can get there themselves. Help the rover reach the crater that has ice inside it.

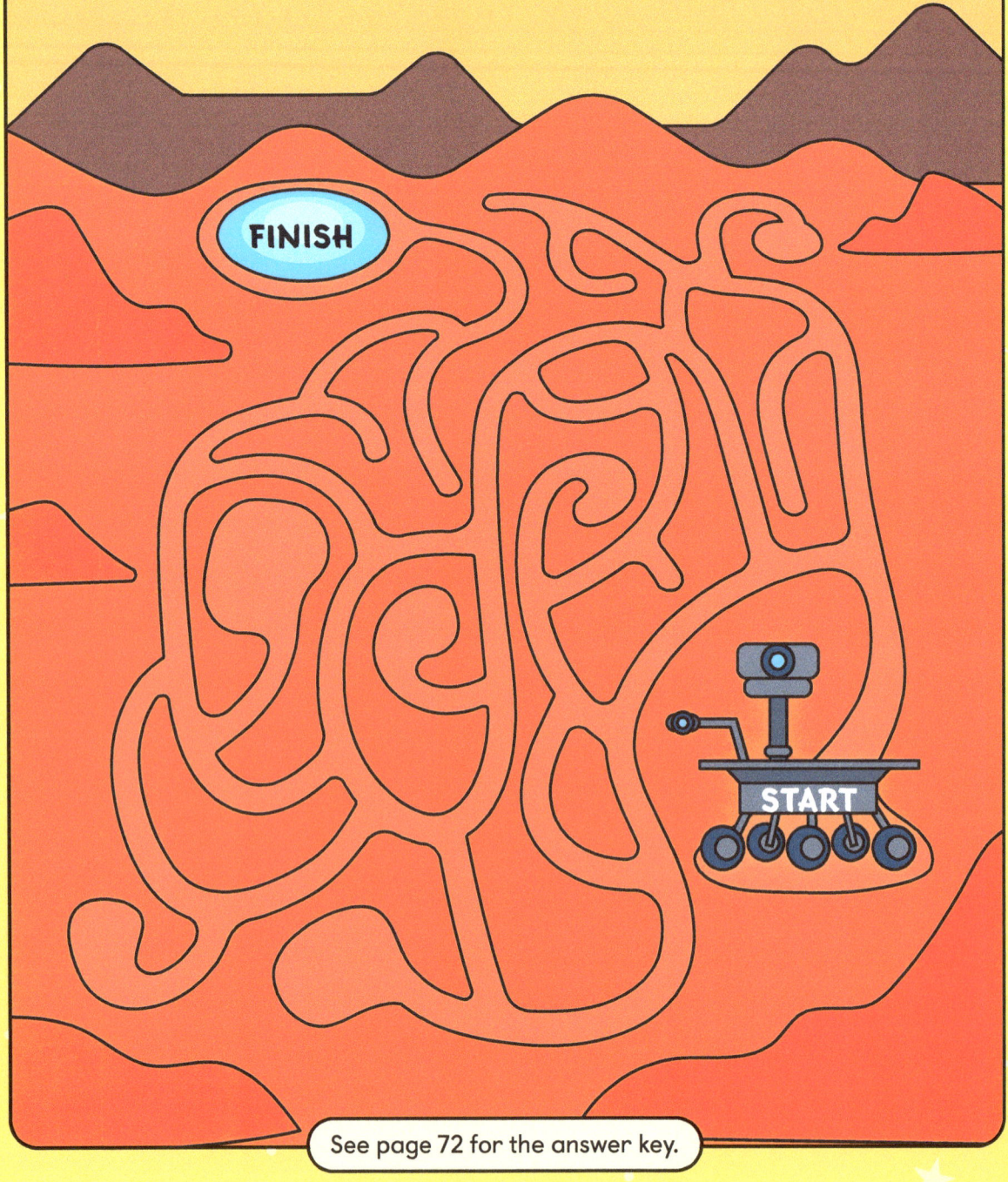

See page 72 for the answer key.

Hey, Look at That!

A planetarium is a theater where images of the solar system are projected onto the ceiling. It can make visitors feel like they are viewing stars, planets, or space travel up close!

Moons Are Special

Our solar system has more than 200 moons. Jupiter has the most moons. Ganymede is the biggest. Circle the moon names in the puzzle. Look left to right, top to bottom, and diagonally.

**GANYMEDE   CALLISTO   IO   TITAN
ENCELADUS   MIMAS   PHOBOS   DEIMOS
CORDELIA   OPHELIA   TRITON**

K	E	P	G	A	C	T	N	F	P	X	C
O	Z	N	B	A	R	H	E	N	H	Q	A
K	O	O	C	I	N	N	R	D	O	L	L
A	V	I	T	E	U	Y	Y	C	B	J	L
Y	B	O	Y	Z	L	Y	M	J	O	O	I
H	N	G	Z	Q	Z	A	N	E	S	P	S
O	T	M	I	L	L	A	D	B	D	H	T
N	A	I	T	M	T	A	N	U	K	E	O
P	W	M	C	I	X	C	U	Z	S	L	I
U	D	A	T	C	O	R	D	E	L	I	A
R	L	S	Q	L	W	L	I	Z	O	A	L
K	V	L	X	D	E	I	M	O	S	J	Y

See page 72 for the answer key.

20

What Is Gravity?

Earth's gravity keeps us and other objects on the planet. The bigger an object is, the stronger the pull.

Dots in the Sky

A constellation is a group of stars that forms a pattern. You can imagine a picture from those stars. Connect the dots to see constellations you might see if you live north of the equator.

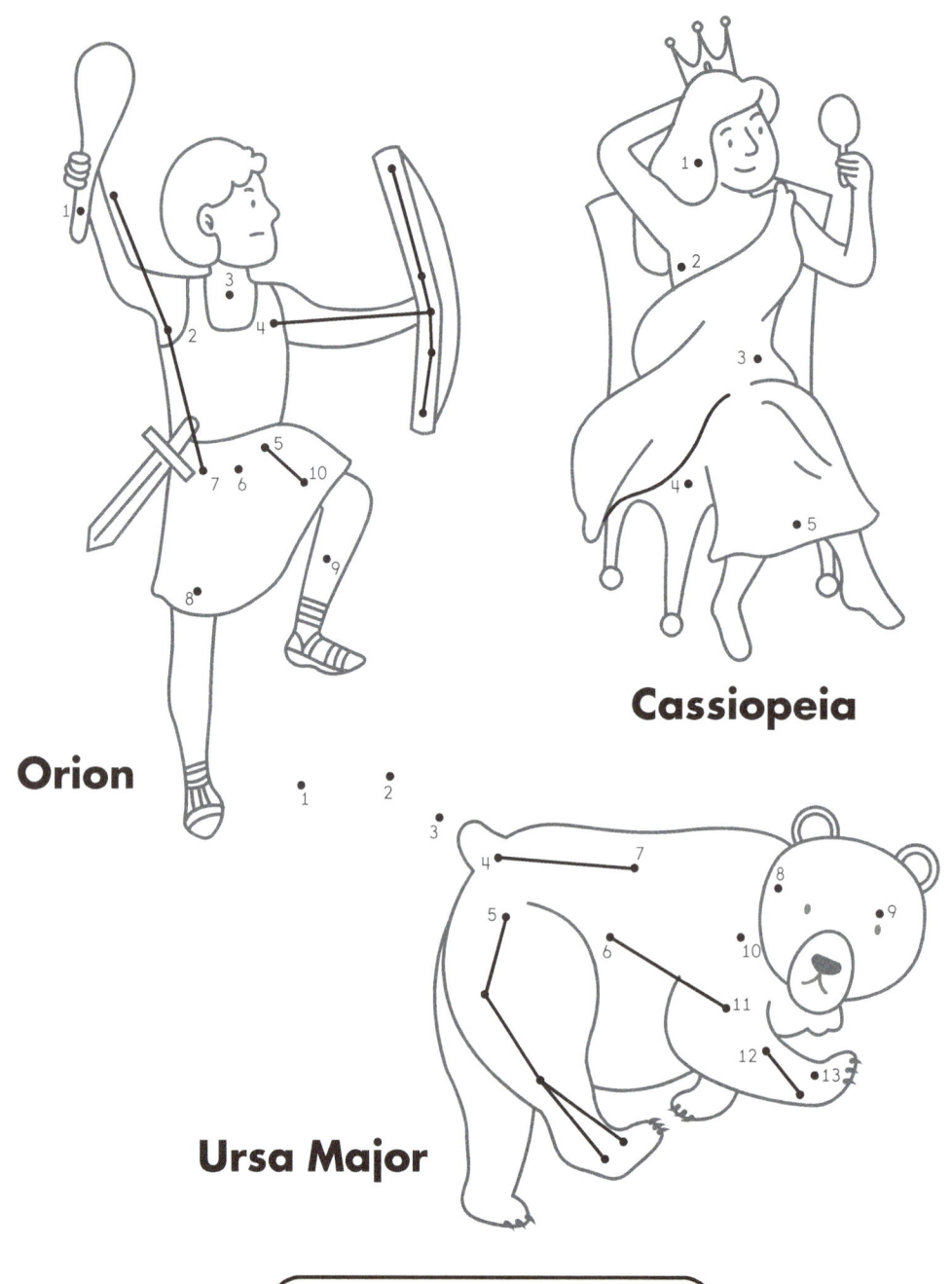

Orion

Cassiopeia

Ursa Major

See page 72 for the answer key.

Magellanic Clouds

Ferdinand Magellan sailed around the bottom of South America. On that trip, he noticed two small galaxies outside of the Milky Way. They are named after him.

Our Solar System

Our solar system has eight planets. Each planet is special. Match the words with the clues to complete the puzzle.

**TILTED   RINGS   HOTTEST   RAIN
MOUNTAIN   SUN   EARTH   LARGEST**

ACROSS

4. Mars has the tallest _____.
5. Saturn has _____.
6. Venus is the _____ planet.
8. We live on planet _____.

DOWN

1. Neptune's _____ is diamonds.
2. Mercury is closest to the _____.
3. Jupiter is the _____ planet.
7. Uranus is _____ on its side.

See page 72 for the answer key.

The Artemis Program

NASA's Artemis program plans to send the first woman and person of color to the moon. Humans have not been to the moon since 1972.

Parts of a Space Suit

Space suits protect astronauts. In space, there is no air to breathe. It can be too hot or too cold. Circle the astronaut suit words in the puzzle. Look left to right, top to bottom, and diagonally.

**HELMET   VISOR   GLOVES   WATER   OXYGEN
RADIO   COOLING   UNDERWEAR   BOOTS**

X	Z	W	T	V	O	X	Y	G	E	N	U
P	A	C	D	L	I	Y	F	T	D	Q	N
H	E	L	M	E	T	S	O	L	N	B	D
C	S	R	E	U	B	O	O	K	G	Q	E
A	O	R	R	P	T	S	S	R	L	I	R
B	I	O	J	S	W	O	W	P	O	K	W
A	O	D	L	I	S	W	A	D	V	H	E
L	C	O	J	I	N	V	T	T	E	W	A
Q	J	B	T	D	N	H	E	P	S	F	R
C	S	Y	Y	S	V	G	R	R	S	L	O
U	R	A	D	I	O	A	T	C	H	C	P
T	V	C	L	A	X	M	M	O	R	M	M

See page 72 for the answer key.

Earth's Tides

The gravity of the moon helps control high and low tides. The sun's gravity plays a part, too.

Water in Space

Saturn's moon Enceladus has an ocean covered with ice. Recently, a burst of water shot out of a crack in the ice. Connect the dots to see what it looked like.

See page 72 for the answer key.

How Fast Does Earth Move?

Earth travels 19 miles (30 kilometers) per second! That's enough to make us dizzy, but we don't feel a thing.

How Scientists Explore Space

Scientists use telescopes to look at space. They also send spaceships with both robots and humans to study things up close. Match the words with the clues to complete the puzzle.

**ROBOT   SPACESHIP   ASTRONAUT   ROVER
TELESCOPE   SPACESUIT   LAUNCH   SAMPLE   ROCKS**

ACROSS
1. A robot that explores a planet
2. A person trained to fly into space
4. To send a rocket into space
6. An astronaut rides in this through space.
8. A tool used to look into space

DOWN
1. A machine doing work for humans
3. An astronaut wears this to walk in space.
5. To collect a small piece of moon or asteroid
7. These things are collected from space to study.

See page 72 for the answer key.

How Our Moon Formed

Many scientists believe that a small planet smashed into Earth billions of years ago. Pieces of our planet flew into space. Those pieces formed our moon.

Sailing Among the Stars

The word "astronaut" comes from two Greek words meaning "star" and "sailor." Help the astronaut get back to the International Space Station from her space walk.

See page 72 for the answer key.

Dwarf Planets

Dwarf planets are smaller than big planets. They are bigger than asteroids. Pluto is one of the biggest dwarf planets. Circle the dwarf planets in the puzzle. Look left to right, top to bottom, and diagonally.

**CERES ERIS HAUMEA HYGIEA MAKEMAKE
SEDNA PLUTO VESTA**

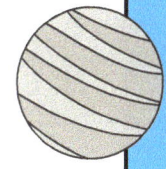

I	E	M	S	O	H	H	B	T
V	I	R	T	R	A	Y	J	D
V	E	U	I	H	U	G	Z	Z
K	L	S	T	S	M	I	B	D
P	W	F	T	B	E	E	D	S
R	O	D	H	A	A	A	S	E
M	I	L	S	A	T	U	G	D
C	E	R	E	S	N	J	X	N
M	A	K	E	M	A	K	E	A

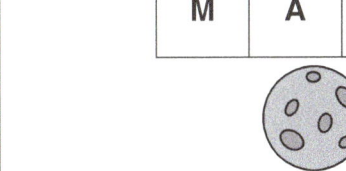
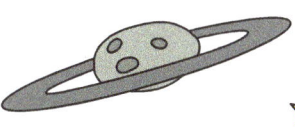

See page 72 for the answer key.

A Helicopter on Mars!

A helicopter the size of a car sometimes flies over Mars. It takes video to help a rover in its search for signs of life. Connect the dots to see what the helicopter looks like.

See page 72 for the answer key.

A Star by Any Other Name

Stars come in all sizes and colors. Blue stars are hot; red stars are cool. Some stars are new, while others are old. This puzzle features different ways to describe stars. Match the words with the clues to complete the puzzle.

**WHITE   ORANGE   DWARF   YELLOW
BROWN   RED   GIANT   HOT**

ACROSS
1. A kind of citrus fruit
4. The opposite of cold
6. The color of apples
8. The color of bananas

DOWN
2. Who Jack met at the top of the beanstalk
3. The color of snow
5. The color of mud
7. Snow White's friend

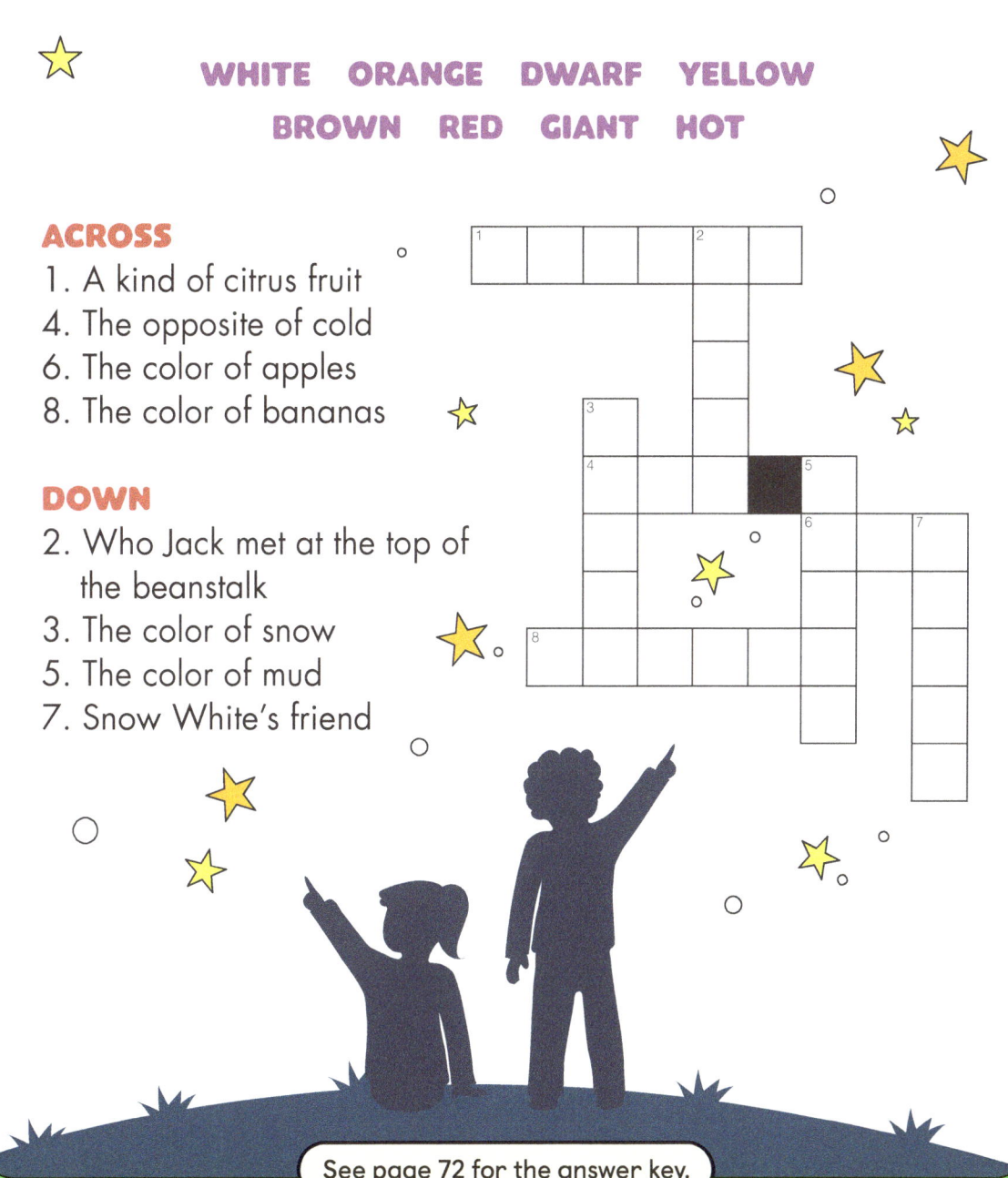

See page 72 for the answer key.

A Belt of Asteroids

Asteroids are rocky objects. They are smaller than dwarf planets. Most asteroids in our solar system are in the asteroid belt between Mars and Jupiter. Help the spaceship make it through the belt.

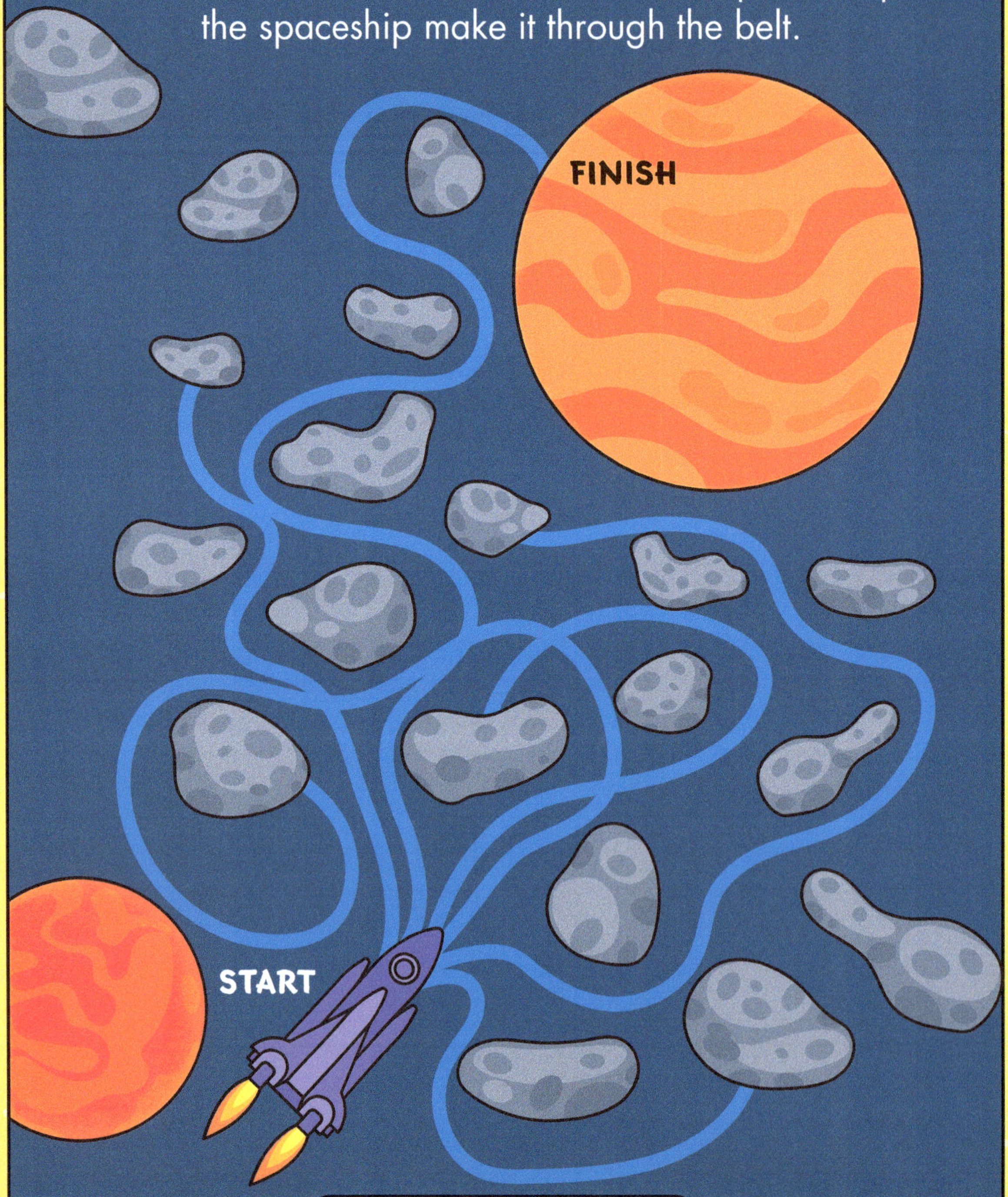

FINISH

START

See page 72 for the answer key.

Can't Catch This Butterfly

Nebulas are clouds of space gas and dust. Many stars start life in nebulas. Some stars explode into nebulas and make unique shapes when they die. Connect the dots to finish one wing of the Butterfly Nebula.

See page 72 for the answer key.

Visible in the Night Sky

There are lots of things you can see in the sky at night. Stars are still in the sky during the day even if you can't see them. Match the words with the clues to complete the puzzle.

**MILKY WAY   ECLIPSE   CONSTELLATION   ORION
STARS   DIPPER   GAS   METEOR**

ACROSS

4. A pattern of stars that makes a picture
7. A shooting star is really a _____.
8. Jupiter is a _____ giant.

DOWN

1. A constellation of a famous hunter
2. Earth is found in this galaxy.
3. The Big _____ is a famous constellation.
5. This happens when the sun's or moon's light is blocked.
6. We can see these twinkle in the sky.

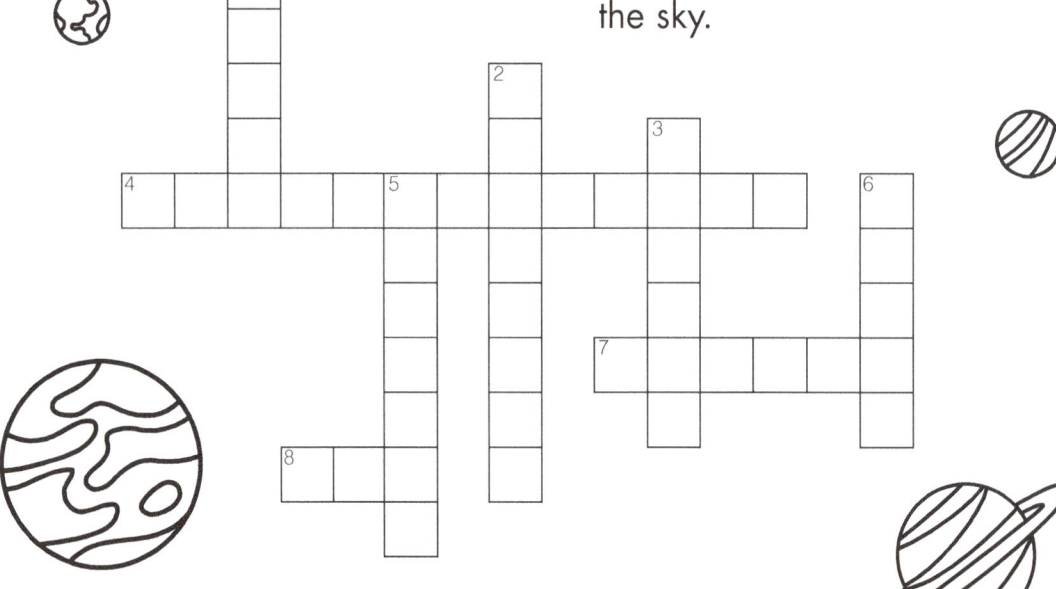

See page 72 for the answer key.

How High Is the Sky?

The sky turns into outer space 6,200 miles (10,000 km) from the surface. Make your way through the airplane before it hits outer space!

See page 72 for the answer key.

Our Home Planet

Earth has three layers: crust, mantle, and core. We live on the crust. Circle the special Earth words in the puzzle. Look left to right, top to bottom, and diagonally.

**ATMOSPHERE   OCEAN   LAND   LIFE   CRUST
MANTLE   CORE   WATER   MOON**

L	A	N	D	E	E	A	K	B	V	X	W
A	P	O	T	L	A	T	J	Y	E	J	N
I	V	M	T	W	D	M	Z	E	W	A	G
R	E	N	O	W	Q	O	E	M	E	C	F
A	A	C	C	O	B	S	K	C	X	R	S
M	O	E	X	T	N	P	O	E	N	U	M
R	T	B	D	V	W	H	W	K	D	S	R
C	O	R	E	R	S	E	A	M	P	T	X
Y	S	E	D	L	T	R	T	S	D	D	N
P	B	H	C	O	I	E	E	X	D	B	C
B	P	Z	G	A	C	F	R	Y	I	D	W
O	F	T	Q	M	Z	Q	E	P	R	M	B

See page 72 for the answer key.

The Apollo 11 Mission

U.S. astronauts first landed on the moon in 1969 with the Apollo 11 mission. Neil Armstrong was the first person to walk on the moon. Match the words with the clues to complete the puzzle.

**FLORIDA   ROBOTS   DUST   CIRCLED
NEIL ARMSTRONG   RAKE   OCEAN   WATER**

ACROSS

3. Before one landed on the moon, a spaceship first _____ it.
4. Missions to the moon launch from this sunny state.
5. Before humans, these were sent to the moon to explore.
6. The surface of the moon is powdery _____.
7. This yard tool was used to collect samples from the moon.
8. The Apollo 11 mission landed in the Pacific _____.

DOWN

1. The Apollo 11 mission did not find this liquid on the moon, but a later one did.
2. This was the first American to walk on the moon.

See page 72 for the answer key.

Will an Asteroid Hit Earth Again?

Asteroids the size of pebbles hit Earth often. Scientists are studying how to bump large asteroids away from Earth. Help the spaceship find its way to the big asteroid heading toward Earth. You can go around little asteroids.

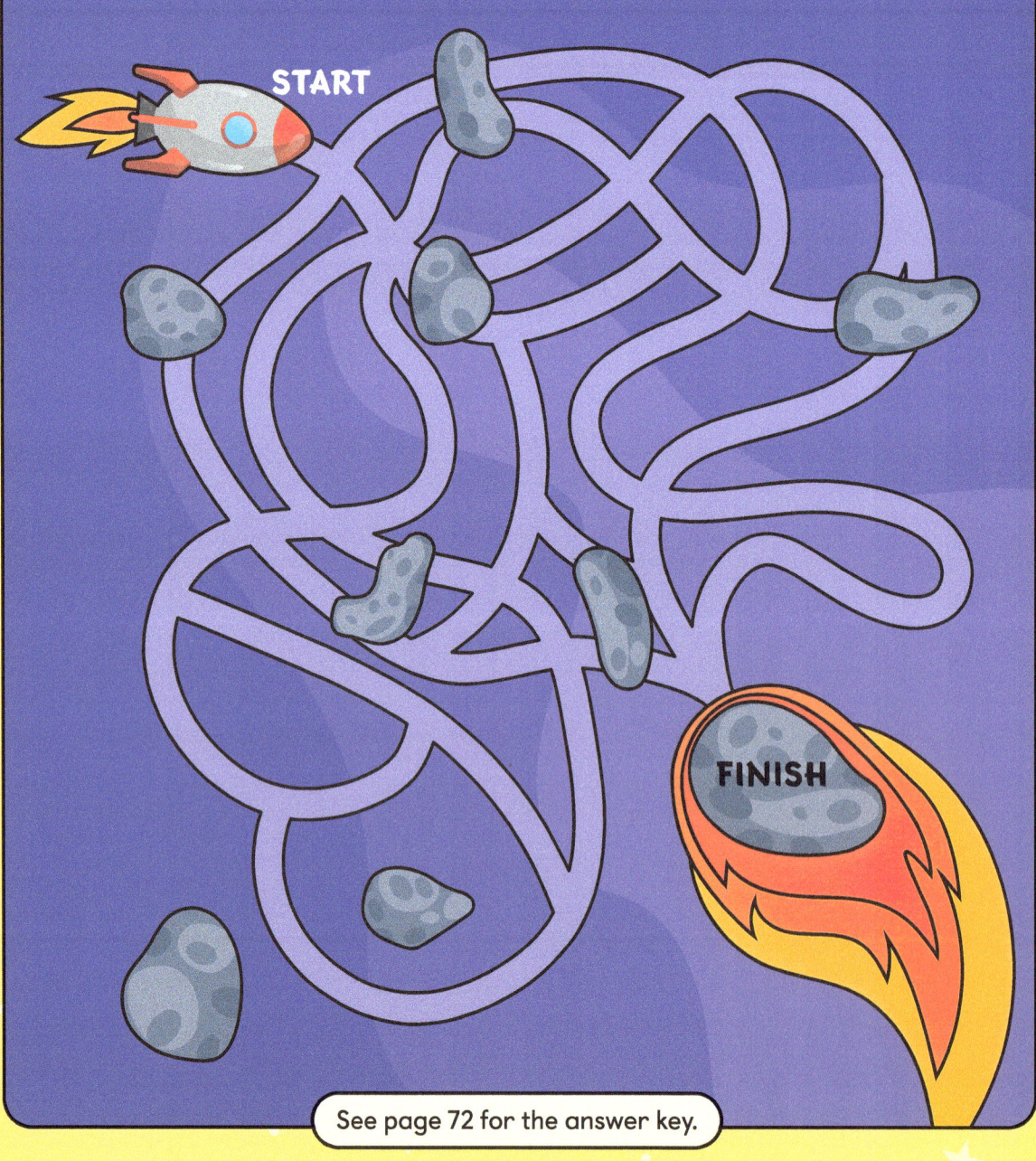

See page 72 for the answer key.

The Swift Planet

Mercury is the smallest planet and moves very fast. It was named after the Roman god of travel and speed.

Brighter than a Star

Venus is the planet closest to Earth. It is the hottest planet, and it shines very brightly. Circle the words that describe Venus in the puzzle. Look left to right, top to bottom, and diagonally.

**EVENING STAR   MORNING STAR   ACID CLOUDS
SISTER   VOLCANOES   MOONLESS   YELLOW**

E	Y	C	I	G	W	G	A	K	S	V	I
I	V	T	X	O	Q	J	O	D	C	O	M
R	U	E	L	R	F	I	U	P	U	L	O
A	R	L	N	F	L	O	G	O	Q	C	R
B	E	K	O	I	L	N	E	I	G	A	N
Y	O	V	Q	C	N	F	S	B	F	N	I
Y	T	R	D	M	O	G	B	Q	T	O	N
W	W	I	F	J	A	T	S	I	S	E	G
O	C	T	O	D	R	G	I	T	L	S	S
A	D	L	F	G	K	V	Y	Q	A	E	T
M	O	O	N	L	E	S	S	R	C	R	A
V	U	W	D	Q	R	S	I	S	T	E	R

See page 72 for the answer key.

The Red Planet

Mars is covered with iron rust and has the tallest mountains. The Romans named the planet after the god of war. Here is one of the rovers exploring Mars.

King of the Planets

Jupiter is the largest planet. It is a gas giant without a solid surface. The Great Red Spot is a hurricane larger than Earth. Connect the dots to find the Great Red Spot.

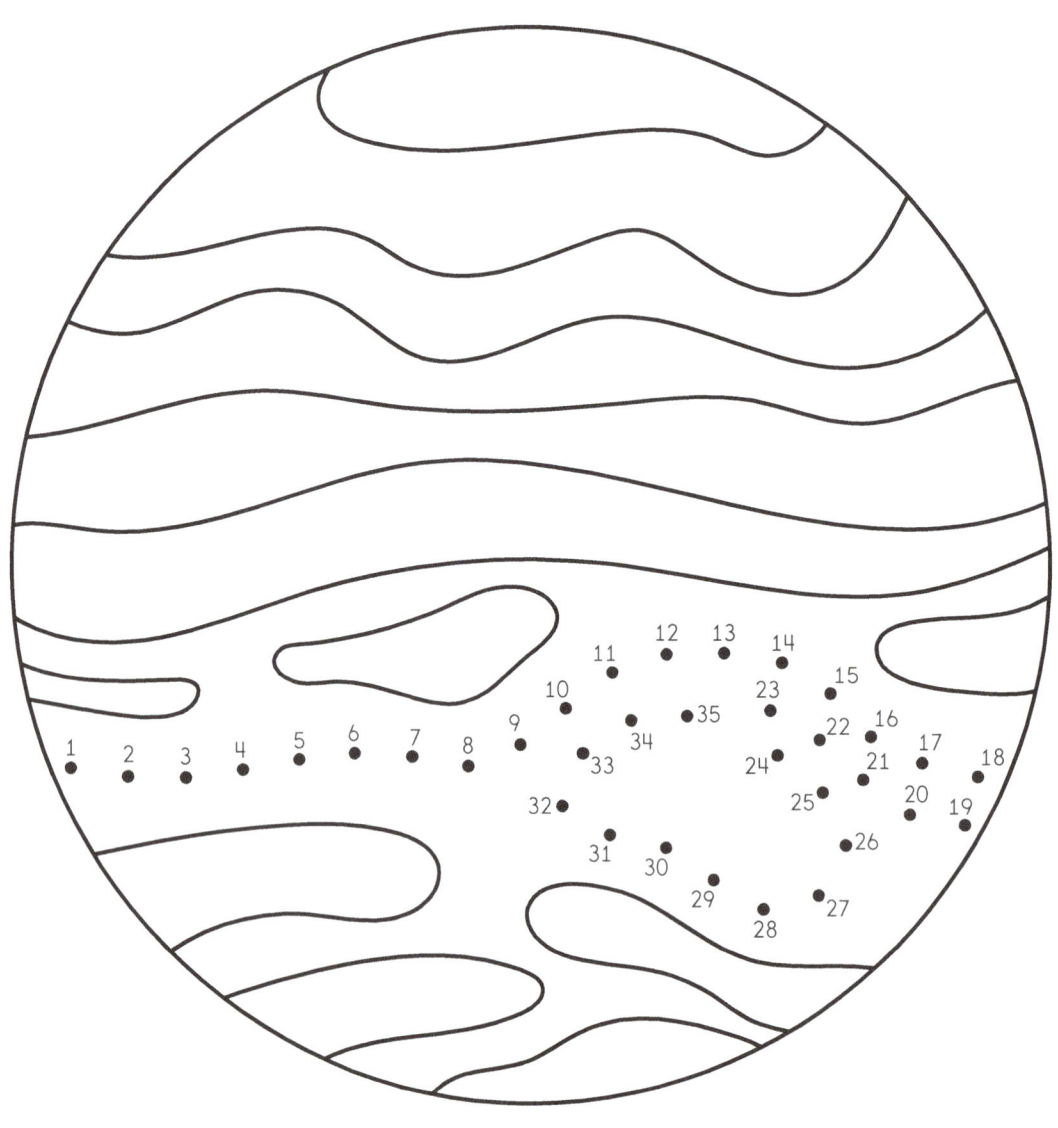

See page 72 for the answer key.

The Jewel of the Solar System

Saturn is famous for its beautiful rings. There are seven main rings and many smaller ones. They are made of ice chunks and rocks.

The Sideways Planet

Uranus is an icy gas giant. It orbits the sun on its side. *Voyager 2* is the only spaceship to fly by Uranus and Neptune. Help *Voyager 2* travel by the planets. Watch out for comets and asteroids.

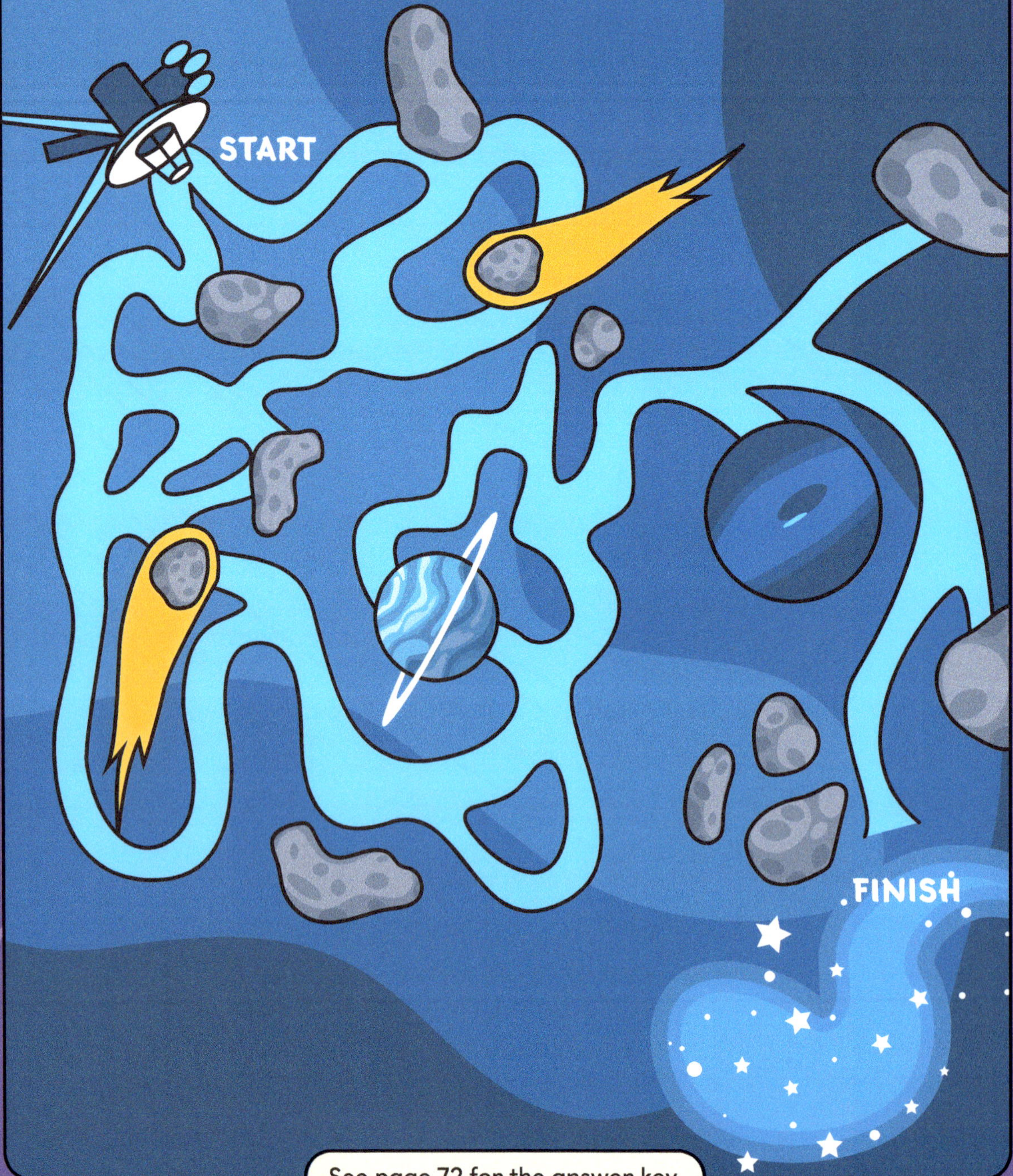

START

FINISH

See page 72 for the answer key.

48

Blue as the Ocean

Bright blue Neptune is slightly smaller than Uranus. It is still 57 times bigger than Earth. The moon Triton is the coldest object in our solar system.

Phases of the Moon

Earth's moon reflects sunshine. The light we see changes as it orbits around Earth and creates moon phases. Circle the moon words in the puzzle. Look left to right, top to bottom, and diagonally.

**FULL   NEW   WAXING   WANING
CRESCENT   MOON   SUN   EARTH**

B	K	D	U	N	F	J	D	C	L
E	L	W	O	V	U	F	I	R	Y
S	A	O	A	I	L	K	P	E	S
F	M	R	O	N	L	P	A	S	Z
B	J	O	T	D	I	W	Q	C	O
Q	P	D	T	H	B	N	W	E	Z
W	A	X	I	N	G	E	G	N	B
S	U	N	M	T	N	X	C	T	G
Z	Q	P	T	Z	F	H	X	W	I
R	C	L	D	C	U	K	X	F	V

  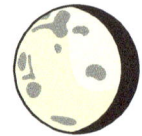 

See page 72 for the answer key.

Black Holes

When a very large star dies, it collapses into a black hole. A black hole's gravity is so strong that even light can't escape.

Horses in Space

The Horsehead Nebula is a favorite of many astronomers. It is near Orion's Belt. Stars are born behind the dark horsehead cloud of gas. Connect the dots to see the space horse taking shape.

See page 72 for the answer key.

Rainbows in the Sky

The human eye sees white light made up of bands of color called a spectrum. When sunlight shines through water in the air, it causes a rainbow.

Things to See from Space

Astronauts on the International Space Station can see some things on Earth. Match the words to the clue to complete the puzzle.

**CANYON   CITIES   PYRAMIDS   DESERT
BRIDGE   RIVER   MOUNTAINS   REEF**

ACROSS
2. Grand _____ in Arizona
3. Himalayas, _____ in Asia
4. Sahara _____ in Africa
6. Big _____ at night

DOWN
1. Great _____ in Egypt
5. Golden Gate _____ in San Francisco
7. Amazon _____ in South America
8. Great Barrier _____ in Australia

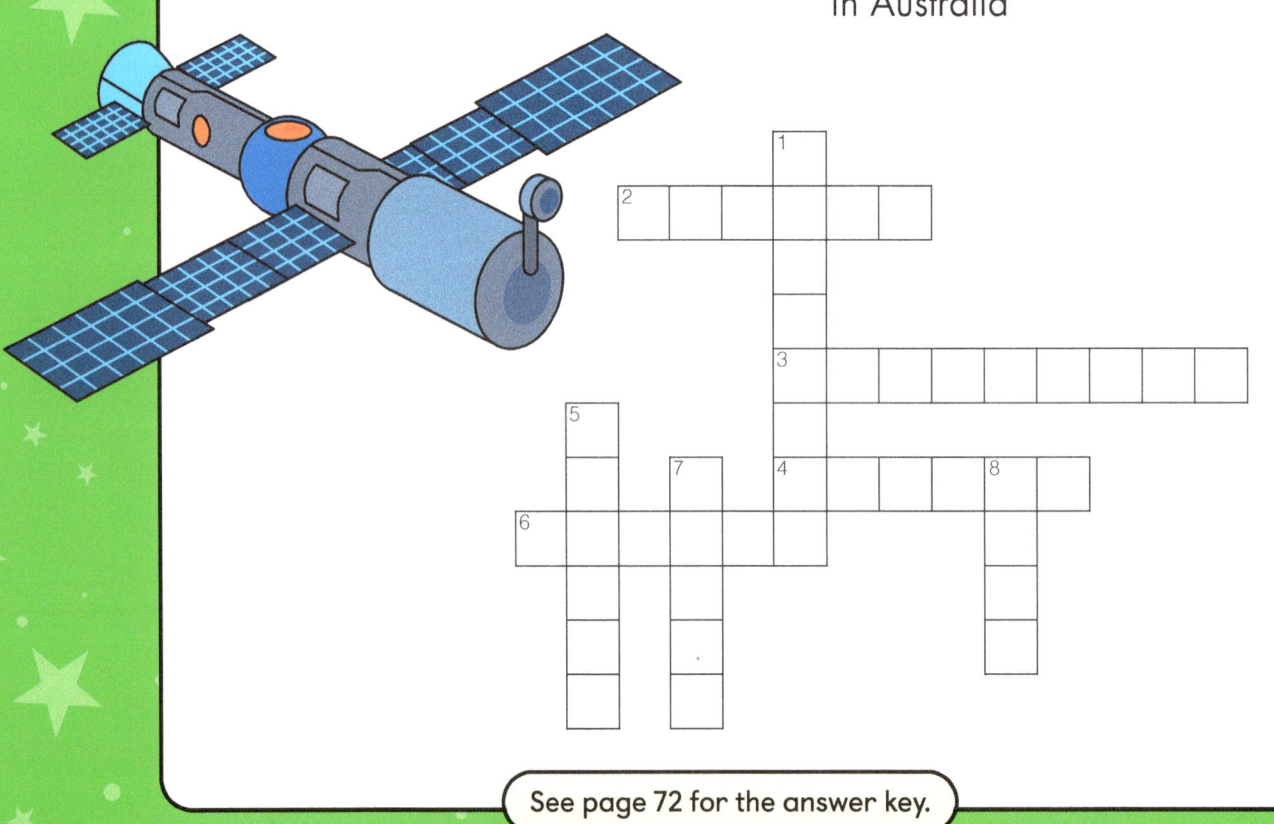

See page 72 for the answer key.

Space Junk

A lot of trash orbits Earth. Space junk is made up of broken satellites, rocket pieces, and astronaut tools and gloves.

Monkeys and Dogs in Space

Animals were sent to space before humans. Sometimes, animals still go to space. Circle the animals that have been to space in the puzzle. Look left to right, top to bottom, and diagonally.

**CHIMPANZEE DOG CAT MONKEY RABBIT
TURTLE FISH FROG INSECTS LIZARD**

C	H	I	M	P	A	N	Z	E	E	Y	X
D	B	E	H	J	M	T	P	O	E	J	H
K	O	Q	H	V	Q	I	U	K	F	Q	Q
I	A	G	U	H	O	X	N	R	X	I	W
X	T	H	Q	S	Y	O	Q	U	T	M	Q
F	V	H	F	Y	M	D	A	A	L	L	C
I	C	I	N	S	E	C	T	S	I	K	E
S	A	Y	M	R	O	R	Q	D	Z	C	K
H	T	L	F	R	O	G	Q	P	A	E	P
L	A	C	N	Z	X	U	V	C	R	T	P
L	Z	P	U	R	V	G	Y	W	D	J	R
E	Y	U	X	R	A	B	B	I	T	F	R

See page 72 for the answer key.

International Space Station (ISS)

The ISS orbits 250 miles (420 km) above Earth's atmosphere. At least seven astronauts are on board at all times.

Southern Constellations

There are 88 constellations in the sky. That's as many as keys on a piano! Hydra is the largest constellation. Connect the dots to see what constellations you might see if you are south of the equator.

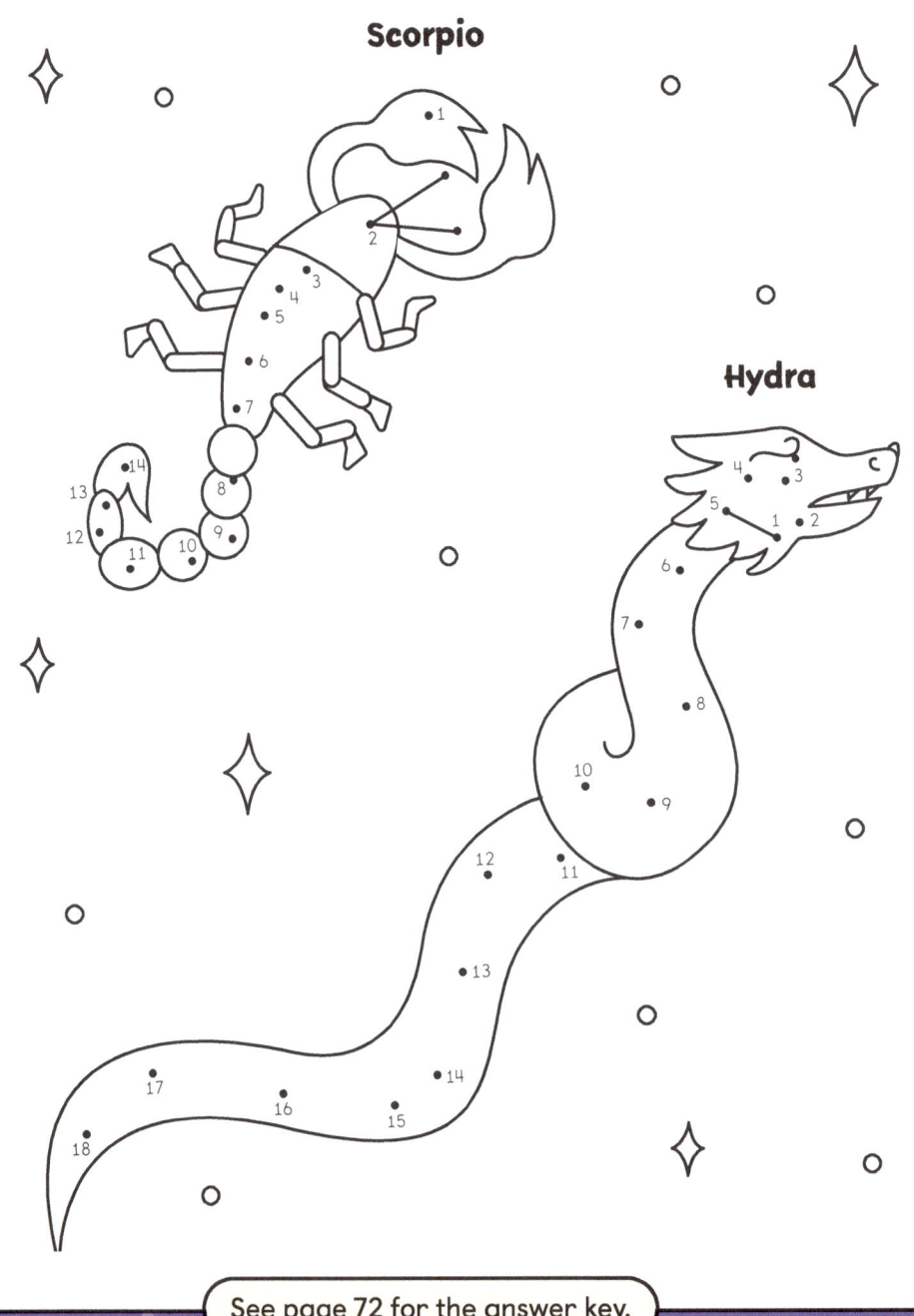

See page 72 for the answer key.

Why Do We See Fewer Stars in the Sky?

City lights at night are called "light pollution." Pointing street and building lights down at the ground would help solve this problem.

Binoculars Reveal Objects in the Sky

Without a telescope, it is hard to see far into the night sky. Still, a good pair of binoculars allow for a close-up view of the moon and some planets. Match the words with the clues to solve the puzzle.

**MOONS   ASTEROID   SATELLITE   PHASES
NEBULA   COMET   CRATERS   VENUS**

ACROSS
2. Crescent and new are _____ of the moon.
4. The planet closest to Earth
6. A large space rock
7. The moon has many of these.

DOWN
1. A star cloud is called a _____.
3. A human-made machine orbiting Earth
5. Many _____ orbit Jupiter.
7. These are sometimes called "dirty snowballs."

See page 72 for the answer key.

Warrior Asteroids

Trojan asteroids are a special type of asteroid. They share an orbit with a planet. Jupiter has the most Trojan asteroids. Earth has only one.

Where Did Earth's Water Come From?

Most scientists think Earth's water came here on asteroids. In the early solar system, many asteroids hit Earth. Some had ice on them. Help this asteroid reach Earth before the ice on it melts.

See page 72 for the answer key.

Montgolfier Brothers

The first human flight was in 1783. The Montgolfier brothers launched a hot-air balloon made of silk and paper. The balloon carried a duck, a rooster, and a sheep.

Sky Snowman

Planets and stars are round, but other space objects are different shapes. One asteroid is named Arrokoth. It is a Powhatan word meaning "sky." Connect the dots to find the shape of the asteroid.

See page 72 for the answer key.

Another Set of Brothers

Americans Wilbur and Orville Wright flew the first airplane in 1903. Just forty years later, the first rockets flew to space.

Light Travels

Light takes time to travel through space. Light from stars takes thousands of years or more before we see it. Match the words with the clues to finish the puzzle.

**NIGHT   LIGHT   SUNBEAM   HEAT
WATER   DAY   FIRE   BRIGHT**

ACROSS

2. A _____ is a ray of light.
4. The moon reflects the sun's _____.
5. After the sun sets, it is _____.
8. A rainbow appears when there is _____ in the air.

DOWN

1. After the sun rises, it is _____.
3. The sun is too _____ to look at directly.
6. Sunlight also brings _____ to Earth.
7. A star is a ball of gas on _____.

See page 72 for the answer key.

Just Right

Goldilocks wanted everything to be "just right." Earth is like Goldilocks. Any closer to the sun and the oceans would dry up. Any farther away and water would freeze.

Do Other Earths Exist?

There are other solar systems in our galaxy. The Kepler Space Telescope has found many planets, called exoplanets. Some of them are the size of Earth. Could they be like Goldilocks, too?

Big Bang

Many scientists believe the universe began with a huge explosion called the Big Bang. That was 13.8 billion years ago. Circle the Big Bang words in the puzzle. Look left to right, top to bottom, and diagonally.

**EXPLOSION   ATOMS   STARS   PLANETS
GALAXIES   GROWING   MOVING   GAS
DUST   LIGHT**

Y	L	U	A	H	G	S	R	M	M	S	O
L	D	I	M	T	T	R	G	Y	G	T	G
K	M	P	G	E	O	Z	O	R	H	A	S
R	T	G	N	H	I	M	T	W	R	R	M
L	V	A	S	G	T	F	S	U	I	S	I
Y	L	G	A	L	A	X	I	E	S	N	M
P	M	B	W	F	K	U	D	U	S	T	G
H	O	E	Z	S	G	C	R	M	U	Q	Q
Y	V	O	P	L	T	A	I	J	U	M	R
U	I	E	X	P	L	O	S	I	O	N	D
M	N	N	J	S	X	M	P	Y	M	G	O
Z	G	L	J	Y	V	Z	J	O	K	T	O

See page 72 for the answer key.

70

Dark as Night

The moon is the right size and distance from Earth to block sunlight. When the moon is in the right spot, it causes a solar eclipse.

ANSWER KEY

Page 2

Page 4
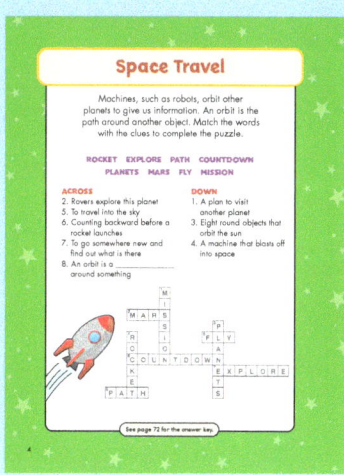

Page 6
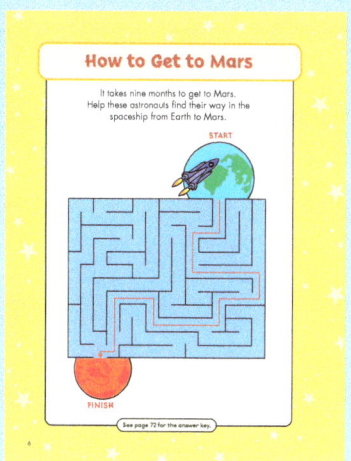

Page 8

Page 10
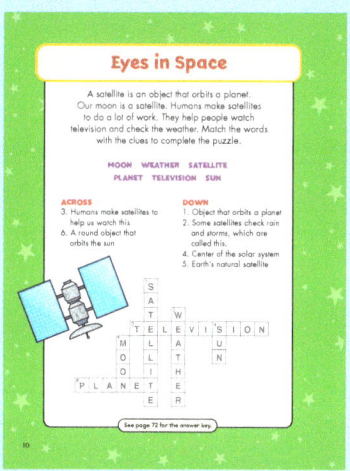

Page 12

Page 14
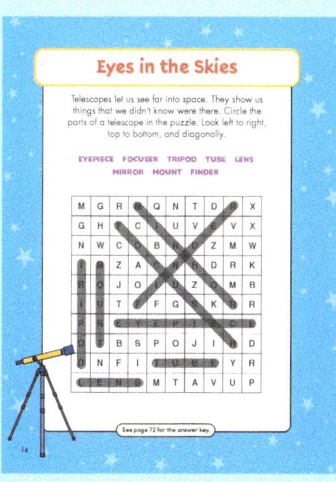

Page 16
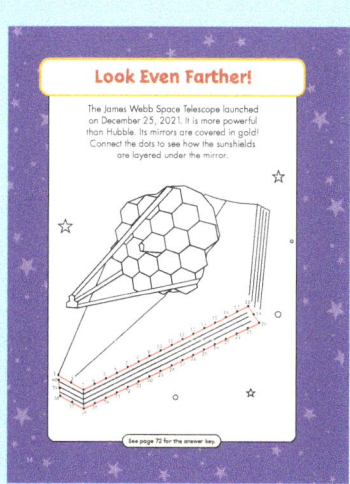

Page 18

Page 20
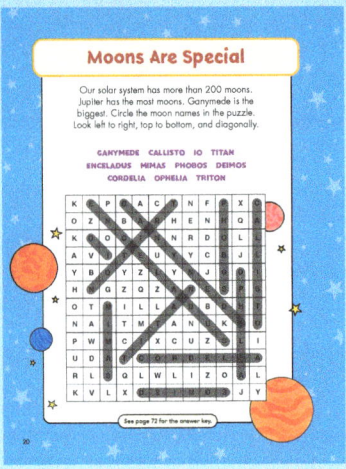

Page 22

Page 24
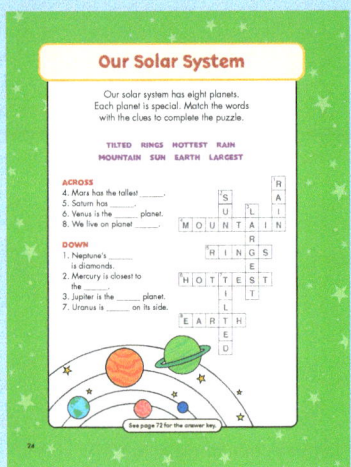

Page 26

Page 28

Page 30

Page 32

Page 33

Page 34
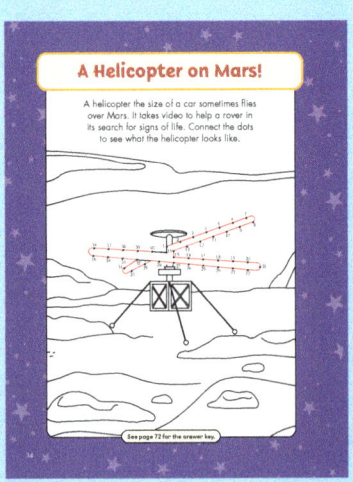

Page 35

Page 36

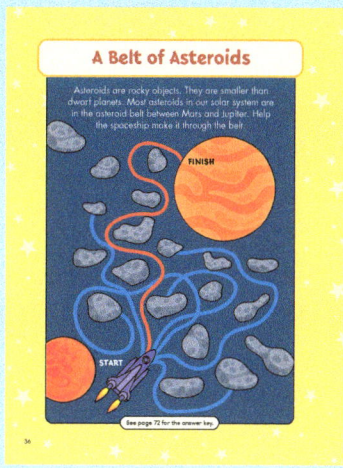

Page 37

Page 38

Page 39

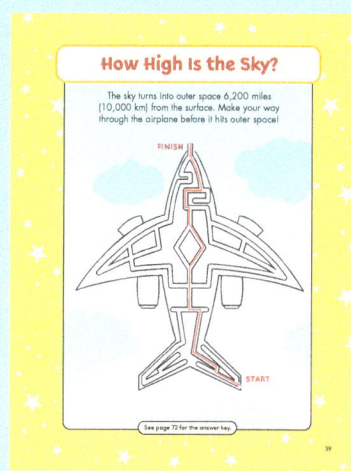

Page 40

Page 41

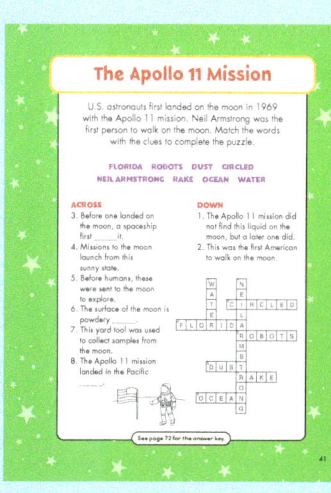

Page 42

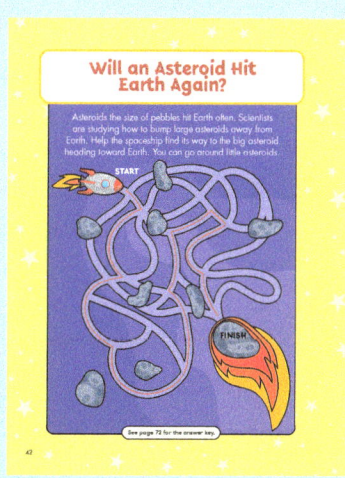

Page 44

Page 46

Page 48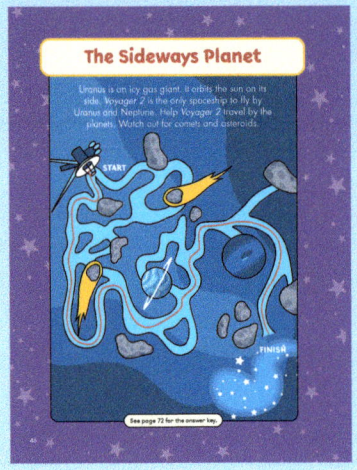

Page 50

Page 52

Page 54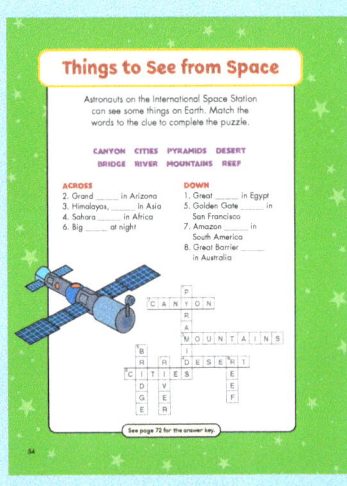

Page 56

Page 58

Page 60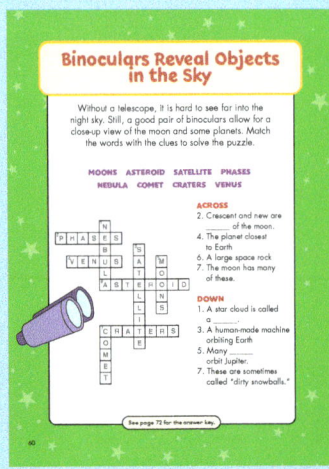

Page 62

Page 64

Page 66
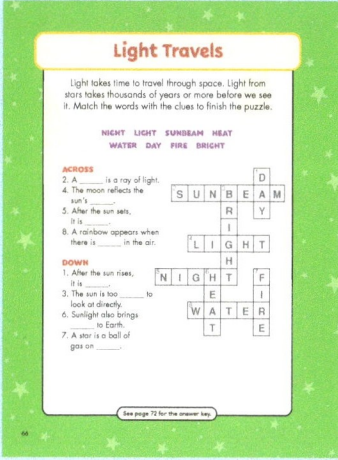

Page 68

Page 70

ABOUT THE AUTHOR

CAP Saucier, a former pediatric nurse, writes about science for children. She authored *The Lucy Man: The Scientist Who Found the Most Famous Fossil Ever!* about Donald Johanson and the fossil Lucy. Her book *Explore the Cosmos Like Neil deGrasse Tyson: A Space Science Journey* tells the story of astronomy. CAP has witnessed both a total solar eclipse and the 2021 launch of the NASA Lucy mission. She is on the board of the Institute of Human Origins. CAP's science writing and adventures around the world earned her membership in the Explorers Club. Learn more at CAPSaucier.com.